Original title:
Echoes of the Ocean Floor

Copyright © 2025 Creative Arts Management OÜ
All rights reserved.

Author: Clara Whitfield
ISBN HARDBACK: 978-1-80587-395-2
ISBN PAPERBACK: 978-1-80587-865-0

Mysteries in the Murky Depths

In the deep where shadows play,
A crab wears shoes, what a display!
Fish in hats swim by with flair,
The octopus clicks, doing hair.

Bubbles dance, the seashells sing,
A dolphin dances, that's the thing!
Seahorses gossip about the tide,
While starfish sit, all wide-eyed.

Reflections in Water's Veil

A mirror fish checks its bright scale,
As turtles race, but none prevail!
Jellyfish float in a wobbly groove,
"Catch me if you can!" they seem to move.

Crabs play poker on sandy beds,
With seaweed snacks and fishy spreads.
Clownfish laugh at their silly fate,
Finding Nemo? Just a traitor's bait!

The Symphony of Submersion

A whale hums tunes undersea,
While shrimp tap dance, oh so free!
Coral plays a pink ukulele,
As fish do ballet, quite un-gay.

Seashells chime as the currents swirl,
A sea lion's toss sends a pearl!
The underwater band, what a show,
With bubbles backstage that steal the glow.

Hushed Stories of the Aquatic Realm

In silence deep, a clam reveals,
The tales of treasure, fancy meals.
Mermaids giggle, hiding their combs,
While sea otters float, crafting their homes.

Crabs tell tales of legendary bites,
Of pirates lost in fishy fights.
The sea cucumber winks, full of jest,
"I'm just a veggie, but I'm the best!"

Dialogues of Drowned Dreams

Bubbles rise, like secrets told,
Fish gossip in colors bold.
One says, 'I've lost my favorite shoe!'
The other laughs, 'I've lost a few!'

In the deep, where laughter flows,
Clams tell tales that no one knows.
A crab winks and says with glee,
'Last week, I danced with a seaweed tree!'

Embraces of the Ocean's Breath

Seashells whisper tales so bright,
Waves tickle sand as day turns night.
A starfish sighs, 'What's that smell?'
'An old tuna sandwich? Oh, what the hell!'

The dolphins giggle, splashing around,
Making waves with laughter, sweet sound.
A jellyfish jives, doing a spin,
'Can I get a partner? Who's diving in?'

Underscore of the Abyss

Down in the dark where shadows play,
A squid tells jokes to keep fear at bay.
'Why don't oysters share their pearls?'
'Because they're busy with their oceanic twirls!'

The deep seeks giggles buried in muck,
While seahorses prance with a little luck.
'What's blue, big, and floats like a kite?'
'A whale on bath day, looking for delight!'

The Depths' Secret Serenade

Anglers fish with hooks and dreams,
Underwater, all's not what it seems.
A fish croons softly, 'Don't take the bait!'
While a turtle grins, 'I'm running late!'

Seas are rich with laughs and lore,
Barnacles giggle on the ocean floor.
'What did the wave say to the shore?'
'Stop crashing on me, I'm trying to score!'

Whispers from the Blue Depths

Bubbles burst with a giggle, a fish wears a hat,
Crabs dance in a conga, imagine that!
Seashells gossip like they're in a café,
Telling tales of the waves that splashed away.

A turtle named Gary stole a snorkel one day,
He swam with the dolphins, what a wild play!
Starfish throw parties on the sandy shore,
While jellyfish boogie, can't ask for more!

Barnacles march in a wobbly line,
Singing how seaweed made great wine!
Octopuses juggle their underwater snacks,
With tentacles flailing, oh, what happy hacks!

The sea turtle grins, with a wink and a spin,
While the seahorse giggles, 'Oh, where have you been?'
Corals chuckle as they sway in a tune,
Dancing to the rhythm of a sunlit afternoon.

Timeless Tales of the Briny Deep

A clam called Clyde told jokes to a lump,
As a whale shot past with a thunderous thump.
He made jokes about pearls and the size of his shell,
While squids served popcorn and seaweed as well.

Deep in the trenches where the funny fish roam,
A dolphin named Daisy claimed she had a home.
"Underwater reality shows just don't fly,
But this coral reef drama? Oh, my, oh my!"

Crabs play charades with a wink and a nod,
Flipping their claws with an air of a prod.
A sea cucumber whispered, "I'm just a blob,
But when I tell tales, the sea creatures sob!"

Giggling squid poured tea from a conch,
As fish in tuxedos made quite the brunch.
The laughter swelled like a wave on the shore,
In a world so absurd, who could ask for more?

Wandering through Water

I splashed on a fish, it gave me a stare,
'The sea's not a pool, are you really aware?'
With bubbles for shoes and a seaweed scarf,
I laughed with a crab as it tried to quarf.

The jellyfish winked, it popped up like gum,
'This party's quite wild, what a splashing fun!'
A sea turtle danced, with a twist and a spin,
Said, 'Dive with a grin, let the games begin!'

The Undercurrent's Song

The eels gathered round, a jamming fest,
With fish on the drums and a clownfish guest.
They strummed on kelp, with such rhythmic cheer,
'We're the band of the brine, come lend us your ear!'

A starfish tapped toes on a turtleneck rock,
While corals burst out in a glittering shock.
With bubbles and laughter, the current did sway,
'We're the undersea stars, come dance if you may!'

Tall Tales of the Deep Blue

A whale claimed a treasure, a chest full of hats,
'They're perfect for dolphins, or maybe some rats!'
With a wink and a splash, they adorned every head,
'The ocean's our stage, now let's go spread dread!'

A squid told a story, oh what a delight,
Of shadows and ships that sailed through the night.
But a lobster shouted, 'That tale's full of fluff!'
'It's better to swim, we've all had enough!'

Voices of the Abyss

The octopus gossiped, its tentacles swayed,
'They fear our weird dance, we're clever and frayed!'
With whispers and bubbles, the deep sea did chat,
A dolphin exclaimed, 'That's a fancy old spat!'

Then came a deep voice, from a grouper nearby,
'Tell me no secrets, I'm just passing by!'
But the clams all erupted, 'Oh, dish us the dirt!'
As the mermaids chimed in, 'You should really alert!'

Lullabies of the Seabed

Underwater giggles swirl like brine,
Fish whisper secrets, all things divine.
Crabs wear pajamas, they dance with glee,
Seahorses sing softly, 'Come swim with me!'

Starfish dream in their cozy beds,
Counting the shells on their wiggly heads.
A dolphin plays piano, a tap-tap-tap,
While octopuses nap in a colorful cap.

Beneath the Surface Still

A turtle's got rhythm, he's doing the twist,
He's got his best buddy, a octopus fist.
Clams roll their eyes and share all the tea,
While jellyfish boogie, oh what a spree!

The sea urchins chuckle, they're prickly but chill,
Their humor's like bubbles, it's sure to thrill.
A pufferfish jokes, 'I'm just full of air!'
Tossing out puns like jelly in the fair.

Voices from the Blackened Sand

Sand dollars gossip, they whisper and spin,
'Did you hear about the crab, he's wearing a pin?'
Anemones laugh with a tickle or two,
While clownfish perform, what a colorful crew!

A sardine bursts in with tales of the tide,
With swimming adventures, he cannot abide.
'Watch out for the netty, it's sneaky and sly,'
Shrimp chime in, 'Bubbly that'll make you cry!'

Tales from the Ocean's Heart

Whales tell tall tales, with flair and a splash,
Of sunken treasures and mermaids that flash.
Octopi duel with their silly old hats,
While shrimps pull pranks on unsuspecting cats.

The plankton party, it lights up the deep,
With glows and groans that'll make you leap.
Sea cucumbers chuckle, they take their sweet time,
In this laugh-fueled world, they dance to the rhyme.

The Abyss' Hidden Archives

In the deep, a clam with dreams,
Holds a treasure of birthday creams.
Shiny pearls and a disco ball,
Throwing parties for fish—such a ball!

An octopus with eight left shoes,
Wonders why he just can't choose.
He dances in his inky suite,
Missing shoes makes it quite a feat!

The seaweed sways to the beat,
A jellyfish gets up on beats.
With bubbling laughter all around,
Their goofy jigs are quite profound.

A crab plays cards with a stingray,
While a whale hums tunes from Broadway.
In the blue they laugh and swirl,
Life beneath is a silly whirl.

Underwater Reveries

A dolphin dons a tiny hat,
Mimicking the sound of a chat.
He tells tales of fishermen's woe,
How they lost their nets and row!

A sea turtle rides a wave,
With a surfboard made of a cave.
He'll catch the best glide with a grin,
While his buddies cheer him from within.

Fish gossip about a bright moon,
That turned out to be a big balloon.
They munch on snacks and giggle loud,
"Is that a star or just a cloud?"

A clownfish juggles seashells blue,
While a seahorse attempts to woo.
Under currents, laughter flows,
In the depths, where silliness grows.

Echoes of the Lost Currents

A whale in a top hat tells jokes,
To a crowd of giggling spoken blokes.
His punchlines float through water clear,
While fishes roll, consumed by cheer.

Starfish throw a quirky party,
Invitations sent out to the party.
With snacks of algae and plankton treats,
All the sea critters move their feet!

A crab's wearing shades, thinking he's cool,
While a pufferfish plays old school.
They start a band under the sun,
With sea-salt rhythms, oh what fun!

Anemones dance with a shrimp so spry,
Floats and twirls—oh my oh my!
In the ripples where laughter gleams,
They sing to the tune of their dreams.

Harmonies of the Hidden

In a kelp forest, a snail sings tunes,
Bopping along to the light of moons.
His shell, a stage, for all to find,
A hidden gig that's just divine!

Barnacles debate the best hairstyle,
Each one claims their look's the style.
While crabs pinch here, and mussels cling,
Their laughter's an unending spring.

A fish in a bowtie says it's formal,
To the seaweed, "Your look is abnormal!"
With flashes of scales and grins so wide,
They all dive deep with goofy pride.

A conch shell holds a raucous chat,
About gossip and the latest spat.
Underwater life's a quirky lore,
Filling the blue with so much more!

Anchored in Silence

Fish in tuxedos dance around,
They wear their scales, oh so profound.
A crab with shades, he struts in style,
While starfish grin, a bit beguiled.

A seaweed band plays tunes on shells,
Their melodies ring like hungry bells.
An octopus juggles sea urchins with flair,
While sea cucumbers have a picnic in the air.

The Forgotten Ballads of the Waves

Seahorses sing in a seaweed choir,
With bubbles of laughter, their voices inspire.
A clam cracks jokes, though no one can hear,
While dolphins roll by, spreading sea cheer.

A pirate fish shouts, 'Yo ho, matey!'
While the stingrays glide, looking all hasty.
The sea foam giggles as tides come and go,
In the underwater bar where sea critters throw.

Beneath the Tide's Gaze

A mermaid lounges, sipping her drink,
While algae carelessly tells her to think.
A grouper plays cards with an old sea turtle,
While the bubbles float up in a gentle hurdle.

The sunken treasure's a real chuckler too,
It laughs at the fish with their old, worn-out shoe.
A shipwreck's ghost tells tales of old woe,
But the jellyfish interrupt with a dazzling glow.

Tales Whittled by Water

Barnacles gather for a storytelling night,
With shrimp as the audience, it's quite the sight.
A whale sings ballads of lost socks and soap,
The fish laugh so hard, they almost lose hope.

A walrus makes puns about freezing the tide,
And all of his friends find it hard to abide.
As bubbles rise up to the surface above,
The ocean's all giggles, it's what they love.

Alignment of Tides and Time

The crab danced a jig, what a sight,
His partner a fish with a tail bright.
Together they twirled in the moon's glow,
Caught in the rhythm of ebb and flow.

The starfish declared it a comedy show,
With jellyfish laughing and putting on a glow.
They flipped and they flopped, all in the sand,
A talent show under the sea, oh so grand!

Murmurs from a Liquid Grave

Deep down where the seaweed grows tall,
An octopus told tales that would baffle us all.
About ships that got lost in the soup of the sea,
And a clam that once sang like a wild jubilee.

The bubbles giggled, creating a scene,
As crabby old sailors turned silver and green.
With tales of the tides and the fish that they caught,
Who knew such funny could be so well thought!

Sirens' Secrets

Mermaids were gossiping over some shells,
Their giggles echoing with splashes and swells.
They talked of a pirate who lost his last shoe,
While searching for treasures, not one but a few.

They flipped their long hair with comical grace,
As seagulls swooped down to join in the race.
While crabs played charades with a wary old eel,
The whole ocean world knew how to make a deal.

The Language of Sand and Sea

Sands told their stories, one grain at a time,
Of turtles that misjudged their own silly climb.
They'd twist in the surf, then slip on a shell,
Creating a scene, oh what a tale to tell!

The waves chuckled softly, rolling in tight,
As sandpipers darted with all of their might.
They tripped over driftwood, oh what a sight,
In the midst of the glee, everything felt right!

Tides of Timeless Whispers

The seaweed dances with a glee,
While crabs play tag, oh can't you see?
A fish with sunglasses, quite the sight,
Says, "Sun's out, fins out! What a delight!"

A dolphin sings a silly tune,
While plankton twirl like stars with a swoon.
"Why don't we surf?" a turtle inquires,
As sea cucumbers cheer like wild choirs.

A mermaid's laugh could make you snort,
She's throwing seashells like a sport.
Fish compete for the funniest face,
As barnacles giggle, losing the race.

Bubbles rise with puns from the blue,
"Why did the starfish float? No clue!"
As waves roll in, the laughter grows,
In this quirky realm where humor flows.

Rhythm Beneath the Foam

Beneath the waves, a party starts,
With jellyfish waltzing, doing fine arts.
A sea horse in a bow tie spins,
"A dance-off time, let the fun begin!"

Octopus drummers keep the beat,
While clams clap shells with happy feet.
Starfish trying to boogie down,
All while wearing their craziest crown.

A crab on stage tells a joke so neat,
"Why don't sea creatures play hide-and-seek?"
The crowd erupts, from turtles to fish,
In this underwater conga line, their wish!

As bubbles pop in a rhythm flair,
Shells are glimmering, a dazzling affair.
The laughter rings from the corals bright,
In this frothy disco under the moonlight.

The Hidden Chords of the Deep

In a sunken ship, a band holds sway,
With rusty instruments, they laugh and play.
A clownfish croons a catchy song,
While sea anemones sway along.

A trumpet made from an old conch shell,
Makes sounds that seem to cast a spell.
"Let's jam!" calls a squid with a grin,
As fish in fedoras dive right in.

A whale bass drops, vibrating low,
As crabs clap claws, putting on a show.
The sea floor shakes with merry tunes,
Lighting up the night with jazz and boons.

"Who needs a stage when you've got the sea?"
A playful dolphin says, so carefree.
In the depths where the rhythms collide,
Life's sweet serenade, they joyfully ride.

Phantoms in the Shallow Waters

In the shallows, a ghostly crab,
Dances around with a silken flab.
"Boo!" he shouts, as fish turn to glance,
"Wanna join my phantom dance?"

An old anchor sways, a creaky ghost,
Who tells tales that make everyone boast.
"In my day, I was quite the catch,
Now I'm here with stories to hatch!"

A seagull swoops, cackling loud,
"Ghost crabs dancing? I'm so proud!"
It's a foolish fest in the bright moon glow,
As shadows leap and ebb to and fro.

Together they laugh, they jump, they jive,
In the shallow waves where spirits thrive.
With each splash, they create a cheer,
In a haunting, funny, watery sphere.

Soliloquies of the Sea Floor

A crab with a hat tells a tale,
Of fish that dance and of snails that sail.
He wiggles his claws, says it's quite the sight,
But all the gossip just gives him a fright.

The clams roll their eyes, say, "Not again!"
"Your stories are silly," they say, "They're plain!"
But the crab gives a grin, so wide and so bold,
"Life's too short, my friends, let the fun be retold!"

A sea cucumber wears fancy shoes,
Swishing and swaying, making his moves.
With fins flipping laughter, the dolphins agree,
"Let's dance till the sunset, wild and carefree!"

So down in the depths where the seaweed sways,
All creatures find joy in their odd little ways.
Laughter and bubbles, a party galore,
On the sandy shore, they create and explore.

Lurking Legends of the Deep

A monster swims by, with a wig made of kelp,
He whispers, "I'm here; I'm much cooler than you felt!"
The clownfish just chuckles, "Oh please, take a seat,
I've seen scarier sights, like my grandma's old feet."

A pouty old turtle claims treasures galore,
"Why, I found a gold pendant, or maybe it's s'more."
But the octopus laughs, "You're quite full of it,
That's just a bottle cap—take a closer look at it!"

The anglerfish grins with his glowing light,
"Even shadows take selfies in my favorite night!"
While the pufferfish pouts, "Don't ruin my vibe,
I'm trying to look big—oh wait, is that a bribe?"

In corners and crevices, tales intertwine,
Of legends so silly, they sparkle and shine.
The depths are alive with mythical cheer,
Where laughter and tales flow like waves without fear.

Glistening Secrets of the Brine

Bubbles burst forth with secrets so bright,
Whispers of clams under shimmering light.
"Did you hear of the fish with a sparkly suit?
He's the latest fashion, so cute and astute!"

Anemones giggle, caught in a whirl,
"Last week, I spotted a pearl wearing a pearl!"
While the seaweed sways, sporting hats on its tips,
Sardines swim by on a raft full of quips.

A lobster plays twister with friends from the bay,
"Left foot on pink coral, now don't go astray!"
They tumble and giggle, in a game of pure fun,
"It's a crustacean party! Come join, everyone!"

So under the waves where the sun softly glows,
With stories and laughter, the humor just grows.
Every tide holds a secret that'll make you burst free,
In the glistening depths of whimsy and glee.

Lament for Lost Ships

Oh, sailboats that drifted, where did they go?
Drunk on the breeze or caught in the flow?
With fish in top hats, and seagulls that squawk,
Their memories linger, like an old sailor's talk.

A buoy sings softly, its heart full of tears,
Recalling the tales of adventurers' years.
"Once, they brought treasures, oh how they'd cheer!
Now they're just echoes, lost far and near."

A lone anchor ponders, "Were we ever so bold?
Did they steal my heart, or just leaves in the cold?"
While barnacles giggle at tales left untold,
"Let's raise a glass to the ships—cheers, behold!"

So here in the waves, amidst laughter and sighs,
The spirit of sailing forever will rise.
We toast to the lost, those whimsical sails,
For every grand voyage, there's joy in the trails.

Secrets in Shells and Stones

A crab in a tux, quite the sight,
He dances on rocks, oh what a fright.
He shimmies with clams, his odd little friends,
While seahorses giggle, the party never ends.

A starfish in shoes, how absurd it seems,
Tap dancing on waves, living out dreams.
With a wink and a grin, he takes to the floor,
While dolphins play tunes we've not heard before.

The seaweed's a curtain, swaying with flair,
As fish put on shows with too much fanfare.
They sport fancy fins, the latest in style,
And planes of hard corals, dressed up for a while.

Oh secrets they keep, beneath shimmering waves,
In shells and in stones, laughter misbehaves.
With giggles and bubbles, they have us in stitches,
In the underwater world, where humor enriches.

Serenades of the Sunken World

A mermaid with braids sings off-key,
To a fish with a mustache, as grumpy as he.
With bubbles for rhythm and seaweed for score,
They charm every barnacle lining the floor.

An octopus juggles, oh what a sight,
His squishy limbs flail, but he's holding it tight.
He trips on a treasure, a shoebox of pearls,
And pirates all giggle at the slapstick swirls.

The turtles roll by in laid-back parade,
Wearing sunglasses, like stars they are made.
With beach balls in tow, and surfboards in tow,
They crash through the currents with laughter and flow.

What sights down below, like a comical show,
Where laughter and bubbles together do flow.
In a world full of whimsy, the creatures unwind,
Creating a symphony, goofy yet kind.

The Depths' Lament

In caves where the angler fish glow with a grin,
They tell tales of goblins who nap on their fin.
With stories of socks that mysteriously sink,
While trying to swim, they tumble and blink.

The sea cucumbers sigh, all slack and resigned,
At the sight of their neighbors' wild schemes unrefined.
They chuckle and snicker at each underwater trick,
As they drift past a clam trying to knit with a stick.

The shipwrecked sailor, with a peg for a leg,
Plays checkers with jellyfish, sitting on a keg.
He claims he was once a suave debonair,
But now he just bumbles, with sea urchins in hair.

Oh, the depths sing a tune of the silly and light,
Where creatures of ocean dive deep into fright.
With giggles and gurgles, they welcome the fun,
In their watery realm, there's no need to run.

Plunge into Silence

A baby whale's pranks, so lively and bold,
Splashing and rolling in waters so cold.
His friends all join in with a splatter and flurry,
While the big fish swim slow, saying, 'Please, don't hurry.'

An old clam with wisdom, sits still and confused,
While seagulls debate if they've all been misused.
With sea slugs in tow, they share salty tales,
Of misadventures where laughter prevails.

The deep sea's so quiet, or so they believe,
Until turtles start sneezing—oh, how they heave!
With shells filled with giggles, they bubble in jest,
Creating a ruckus, a curious quest.

So plunge into silence, where silliness thrives,
In the depths of the ocean, where humor survives.
With creatures at play, and antics galore,
Beneath all the waves, there's never a bore.

Resonate in the Blue

Bubbles laugh like popcorn thrown,
Starfish dance when sand is blown.
Crabs hold court on tiny thrones,
While dolphins joke in playful tones.

Seashells gossip with each wave,
Telling tales of brave and naive.
Octopus painting with no brush,
In their art, there's quite the hush.

Goldfish gossip in schools so bright,
As sea turtles glide, just out of sight.
Anemones wave, hilarious sights,
As laughter erupts through ocean heights.

So let's splash in this watery spree,
Where humor swims wild and free.
In this realm beneath the brine,
The fun here is simply divine!

The Deep's Distant Call

Whales sing wacky tunes of yore,
As jellyfish twirl and soar.
Clownfish chuckle at jokes untold,
While sea urchins tease, feeling bold.

A lobster wearing a tiny hat,
Declares he's the king of this habitat.
Crabs doing the cha-cha on the floor,
Making sure to show off their score.

Seahorses giggle in pairs so neat,
As waves come crashing, a silly beat.
Coral reefs blaze with colors so grand,
It's a vibrant circus from seabed to sand.

So dive down deep, have a good cheer,
For laughter is found in waters so clear.
Each ripple and splash holds a punchline rare,
In this underwater realm, there's joy everywhere!

Reverberations of the Sea

A walrus wearing shades debonair,
Sips iced tea with a nonchalant air.
Clams are gossiping about the tide,
Snapping shells in sheer, giddy pride.

Starfish count their arms in a race,
While sea cucumbers roll at their pace.
Fish throw a party, a finned parade,
With slippery moves that never fade.

A grouper gets stuck in a net of jokes,
While a school of mackerel tease like folks.
Turtles make puns as they amble slow,
In this quirky ocean, laughter's aglow.

So heed the call of the tidal ballet,
As funny frolics whisk worries away.
Under the waves where the silliness flows,
Life's just a comedy that endlessly grows!

Chants of the Forgotten Coast

A seagull yodels, a pirate's delight,
While crabs dance a jig, what a sight!
Sunken ships with tales of the blunder,
Whisper of treasure and humorous thunder.

Oysters hold court with pearls of wit,
Sharing tall tales as the tide allows it.
A dolphin's backflip gets a loud cheer,
Fins waving proudly, buoyed with good cheer.

Barnacles cling to ancient wood,
Recounting adventures like they should.
A squid pulls faces, ink splats fly,
In this sea of laughter, we all comply.

So come along to this coastal spree,
Where every wave holds a giggle, you'll see.
From the depths to the shore, let joy unfurl,
In the waters of humor, the whole world twirls!

Voices from the Maritime Silence

Bubbles float up with a giggly cheer,
Fish laugh at seaweed, their tangled hair.
Crabs tap dance on barnacles so bright,
While jellyfish float, glowing soft in the night.

Starfish, on rocks, throw a quirky ball,
While an octopus plays hide-and-seek in the hall.
Seagulls squawk loud, a raucous crowd,
But down on the floor, they're not so proud.

The catfish wear hats, such a silly sight,
While seahorses trot by, oh what a fright!
Everyone's laughing, what a fishy show,
As the tide rolls in, and the seaweed grows.

In the waves, the stories swirl and spin,
Of a clam with a shell that's way too thin.
Under the surface, hilarity brews,
As the ocean sings out its whimsical blues.

The Underwater Reverie

Clams tap dance to a beat unheard,
With snappy shells, they spread the word.
Fins flit by like they're in a race,
While lazy turtles adopt slow grace.

Mussels gossip as the currents sway,
Sardines flash bright in a silver ballet.
A playful dolphin juggles seaweed strings,
And a walrus claims he's got the best bling!

Cranky lobsters wave their pincers wide,
As the pufferfish puffs up with pride.
Underwater antics, oh what a scene,
Where every creature is fit for a queen.

The sea is alive with giggles and glee,
A treasure trove of wittiness, you see.
Grumpy old fish, they just can't compete,
With the comedic charm of the ocean's heartbeat.

Secrets of the Forgotten Blue

In the deep, a whale sings a silly tune,
As squids swim chaotically under the moon.
Coral reefs giggle, their colors ablaze,
While colorful fish join in the craze.

A clownfish frowns in a bubble of doubt,
Claiming his jokes have been worn out.
But a wise old eel coaxes him near,
Saying, "Come on now, we're all here to cheer!"

A sneaky sea urchin guards a big pearl,
His jokes are sharp, like his spiny swirl.
But hey, what's this? A hermit crab's hat!
That's the best punchline—imagine that!

All around, the laughter dips and dives,
Amidst the seaweed, joy truly thrives.
In the depths, the silliness knows no bounds,
As the ocean giggles with magical sounds.

Mysteries in the Aquatic Silence

A dolphin tells tales of a bubble parade,
While crabs make sculptures, all hand-made.
Starfish play chess in the sands of the shore,
While sea turtles roll, yearning for more.

Sharks swap stories, a little too bold,
Of the great big fish that each one sold.
The grouper grins, hiding tales of his own,
Of the treasure he found where the seaweed has grown.

Anglerfish chuckle, their lights flicker bright,
While octopuses juggle with all of their might.
A conch shell's a phone, so call and declare,
"Who's the funniest fish? Come and compare!"

Down in the quiet, there's a raucous delight,
With secrets and jokes that the currents ignite.
Swimming and laughing, with charming finesse,
In the depths, the laughter—oh, what a mess!

The Depths' Quiet Resonance

Bubbles rise and fish do dance,
They think it's just a mermaid's romance.
Crabs take selfies in the sand,
While sea cucumbers join a band.

Starfish wear the latest trend,
With clam shells they do recommend.
Anemones giggle at the show,
As seaweed sways, a wiggle flow.

Octopus makes a hearty stew,
While shrimp play cards in shades of blue.
The whale hums a jazzy tune,
As dolphins slip beneath the moon.

In this deep world, we find delight,
Where every fin has quite a bite!
So laugh with glee, 'neath waters wide,
For under waves, fun does abide.

Elegy of the Silent Waves

The seashells gossip, oh what a chatter,
They laugh at crabs who just can't patter.
Sand dollars counting their treasure loot,
While tangled seaweed grows quite a hoot.

Seahorses twirl, in fanciful suits,
Planning a party with jellyfish flutes.
A big fish parties, he's quite the sight,
Dancing with sharks, oh what a night!

The squids tell tales of sailors past,
With ink and giggles that hold them fast.
"Join us for fun!" they tease the stars,
While rays glide by in laser cars.

Yet, here they bide, in silent waves,
With laughter hushed, they play in caves.
In water's arms, they find their cheer,
Making waves of joy, ever clear.

Whispers of the Deep

Underwater puns float through the blue,
Where fish wear hats, and sometimes shoes.
Turtles giggle at jokes untold,
While clowns of the sea make their bold.

Guppies swim in a synchronized line,
Flipping and flopping, they do just fine.
A walrus winks, with a beard so grand,
He's the life of the party, don't you understand?

A pufferfish joins in for kicks,
With laughter that's sharp, just like his tricks.
Corals cringing at every jest,
While anemones wiggle, feeling blessed.

Dolphins launch into flips so wild,
Nature's comedians, every child!
So next time you fret, dive down and see,
The deep sea's humor—it's as real as can be!

Secrets Beneath the Tide

Beneath the surf, the fish plot plots,
They joke about sailors' empty pots.
A flatfish claims he's got the moves,
While a lone sea snail just grooves.

An octopus with eight left feet,
Can't seem to find the right dance beat.
But when the plankton throws a ball,
The giddy sea life has a ball!

Crab bandmates strum on shells so sweet,
While the seagulls dance to the beat.
With algae as their confetti fling,
They celebrate the crown of spring.

And as tides shift, the jokes flow free,
Water's laughter, a jubilee!
So while we float on ocean's tide,
Remember the giggles where secrets hide.

The Ocean's Embrace

Down below where seaweed glows,
Crabs in hats strike silly poses.
A fishy dance, a wiggly jig,
While jellybeans float, oh so big.

Treasure chests filled with lost socks,
Shy octopuses do the moonwalk.
Bubble-blowing whales have a blast,
While starfish giggle, they're unsurpassed.

Mermaids laugh at fishy jokes,
Every wave a stretch for folks.
Clams play cards, it's quite a sight,
Shimmering shells under the moonlight.

So dive right in for jolly fun,
In the deep blue where mischief's spun!
An underwater carnival awaits,
Freed from gravity, let's celebrate!

Abyssal Melodies

In the depths where shadows play,
Sea cucumbers sway all day.
Cranking tunes on seashells rare,
Mermaids strum with salty flair.

Dancing fish in goofy grace,
Wink and twirl in a water race.
Bubbles pop like silly tunes,
As clams jive beneath the moons.

Comical crabs form a band,
While starfish shake, oh so grand!
Tangled seaweed, they try to twine,
"Ooops, I tangled, entwined divine!"

Jellyfish float, quite out of tune,
Yet all join in for a cartoon.
The deep blue sings of life so bright,
A laughter-filled dive into the night.

Glittering Tales from the Gloom

In the shadows, where tales weave,
Fishes gossip, oh do believe!
Mermaids share the latest trend,
"Should we wear shells or just suspend?"

A treasure map made with old cheese,
Forgotten snacks, oh what a tease!
The angler fish with woven lights,
Calls out for midnight snack delights.

Seahorses race on bubble steeds,
Shouting loudly, "We're the weeds!"
Court jester turtles roll on by,
Cracking jokes that make us sigh.

Glimmers flicker in the dark,
Fishy snap selfies, like a lark.
So tell me more from depths below,
Of glittering tales that steal the show!

Tidal Echoes Unheard

Waves crash down with silly sounds,
Seagulls mimic, jumping bounds.
Fish wear sunglasses, looking cool,
Flipping tails, they rule the school.

Octopus chefs whip up a feast,
Dancing around like a strange beast.
"Order up!" they call and cheer,
"I'll take a brew, make it clear!"

Whales play tag, all in a rush,
Splashing around, what a big hush!
Sea turtles giggle, lost on the chase,
"What's that? A crab in a bowtie face?"

Sandy castles grow tall and bright,
While clowns of the ocean take flight.
Beneath the waves, the fun doesn't end,
In a world where all are a friend.

Songs of the Forgotten Marine

Bubbles rising, fish in a race,
A crab's cranking jokes with a charming face.
Seashells sing softly, off-key they croon,
An octopus lost in his polka-dot tune.

Jellyfish jive with a dance so bizarre,
A dolphin giggles, steals a sea star.
Turtles play chess with a coral reef set,
Splashing and laughing, no hint of regret.

Starfish recite all the stories of yore,
Conch shells trumpet stuck inside a door.
Anemones smile, wave their arms in delight,
While seahorses chomping on seaweed take flight.

Ocean's a circus, all layered in blue,
Mermaids do cartwheels, what more could they do?
The sea floor's a stage, with no need for fame,
Just laughter and joy; it's a bizarre game.

Depths of the Silent Realm

Down in the quiet, where crabs try to sing,
A clam yells, 'Shh!' like it's the real thing.
Fish in a chorus, forget the main tune,
They'd rather just giggle and float 'round a moon.

Squid with a pencil draws cartoonish stuff,
Mystery bubbles—oh, are they too tough?
Starfish debate how best to get baked,
Their wit is a dessert, delicately flaked.

Deep in the shadows where sea cucumbers dwell,
They play hide and seek; oh, do they do well!
Mollusks exchanging their tales of the deep,
While dolphins chuckle and take a big leap.

A treasure trove filled with the quirkiest finds,
Worn-out old jokes and fish with big minds.
Under the surface, the pranks never cease,
In a realm full of giggles, swimming in peace.

The Abyssal Whisper

What's that lurking down in the gloom?
A sardine chorus with a tuba and broom.
The flatfish are flapping and trying to hide,
Playing peek-a-boo, full of fishy pride.

Mussels at midnight with stories to share,
Discussing the latest in seaweed hair.
Nudibranchs gossip about who wore it best,
Their colors are vibrant; oh, what a fest!

A sunken ship's parrot squawks nonsensical rhymes,
And sea urchins argue over glittery limes.
An angel fish flipping through channels of sea,
While a grouper joins in, "Just let it be!"

In the dark waters, laughter will brew,
Each whisper a jest, as they rave and renew.
Beneath all the waves, there lies a surprise,
A party so wild, even plankton can rise.

Tales from the Gloomy Below

Deep in the murk, where the rays rarely shine,
A whale tells a tale about dining on brine.
His friends roll their eyes, with a flick of a fin,
"Do tell us again, how you slept on a pin!"

An angler fish glows, trying hard to impress,
But the rest are just laughing; what a big mess!
Sea sponges are busy with cleaning their clothes,
While jellyfish crack up with their tentacle prose.

Cranky old catfish complains 'bout the noise,
"Back in my day, we had much better toys!"
While everyone chuckles at stories of yore,
Their laughter resounds from the ocean floor.

So here in the depths, where the sunlight's a tease,
The quirkiest humor brings everyone ease.
In this watery haven, with fishy delight,
Each tale is a treasure, and jokes take their flight.

Harmony of the Lost Depths

In the gloom, a crab did dance,
With wheels and fins, he took a chance.
Seaweed wigs, they waved so high,
As dolphins giggled by and by.

A squid in shades, oh what a sight,
Played poker with a fish at night.
The shipwreck's ghost, a jolly sailor,
Told jokes so bad, they'd make you wailer.

Octopus twins made jelly stew,
While turtles cheered, 'Oh, taste this new!'
Clams sang songs of sand and clay,
Unaware that they had lost their way.

So next time you dive deep and roam,
Remember the fun beneath the foam.
The sea is silly, don't be forlorn,
Where laughter blossoms, and dreams are born.

Serenade of the Dark Waters

In murky depths, a party brews,
With fish in hats and drunken blues.
A whale's trumpet, loud and grand,
Drew in a crowd from every strand.

Starfish played tambourine with style,
While squids served shots, they cheered a while.
The pufferfish burst from joy or dread,
Leaving all scales with jokes instead.

A seahorse DJ spun the tunes,
With shrimp on stage, they made cartoons.
A jellyfish glowed like a disco ball,
In dark waters, they'd have a ball.

So dive beneath, join the jest,
Where bubbles pop and fish are dressed.
The silly sea, it bounces and flows,
With laughter that nobody knows.

Legends from the Mystic Deep

A mermaid sang with a voice so sweet,
Her chorus drew in fish for a treat.
But they just snickered, swam right past,
For seaweed was stuck on her hair so fast.

An octopus spoke, with tales so tall,
Of treasure maps and a giant, gray moll.
But he tripped and fell, lost his cool,
Knocked over a clam, declared he's the fool.

The crab rolled dice on a treasure chest,
Claiming 'This life, surely the best!'
Then flipped it open, found just a boot,
Laughed at his luck, 'Well, isn't this cute?'

With each dive deep into tales they weave,
Hilarity lurks in the depths, believe.
So when you hear them, don't be a prude,
Join in the laughter; it's truly good food.

Reverberations from the Shells

Shells conspired beneath the foam,
Creating sounds that felt like home.
Fernando the clam, a dance so neat,
Moved his shell to a rhythmic beat.

Mussels chimed in with a clatter,
In the depths, silly dreams would splatter.
The starfish laughed, 'This groove is grand!'
As plankton swirled, they formed a band.

A conch trumpet blared, loud and proud,
Summoning fish, joyously bowed.
The sea cucumber rolled with flair,
Wiggled and giggled, without a care.

So remember the laughter down below,
In the world where chuckles flow.
With shells that giggle, and currents that sway,
The ocean's humor is here to stay.

Ripples of Long-Lost Stories

In the deep, where fish wear hats,
Old tales swirl, like swimming cats.
Crabs narrate their snappy fights,
While seals tell jokes with all theirmight.

Starfish roll their eyes and groan,
As clams throw shells, it's quite a tone.
Octopus plays cards with glee,
While turtles swim, so gracefully.

The seaweed sways to every chuckle,
Creating laughter, a gentle buckle.
Barnacles join the fun-filled spree,
As dolphins flip with joyful glee.

In coral reef, the puns abound,
As laughter echoes all around.
From depths so dark, to light so clear,
These tales of joy we always cheer.

Fables from the Sea Floor

A hermit crab with a tiny home,
Complains, "Why can't I roam and roam?"
A jellyfish with a glowing charm,
Says, "My shine can't cause you harm!"

Mollusks tell their tales of grace,
As sea urchins don their spiky face.
The anglerfish boasts of its light,
"It's not my size that gives me fright!"

The narwhal plays a trumpet tune,
While fish dance round in leafy swoon.
"A treasure's found!" the seahorses sing,
"Wait, it's just a lost old ring!"

The sand dollars roll with laughter loud,
Celebrating under the seaweed shroud.
With a wink and splash, the tales are spun,
In this funny realm, it's all good fun.

Whispers from the Twilight Depths

In the twilight where shadows creep,
The fish start gossiping, secrets to keep.
"I saw a diver!" whispered the bass,
"Maybe he wanted to join my class!"

The squid tried to play a game of tag,
But ended up stuck in a plastic bag.
"I should've known!" the sea cucumber sighed,
"Fun in the depths—let's not be tied!"

The seniors of the reef spin tales so grand,
Of mermaids brushing through the sand.
But all the young fish roll their eyes,
Saying, "Those stories are full of lies!"

As bubbles burst with jubilant sound,
The humor flows freely all around.
With fishy giggles and playful leaps,
These twilight whispers hold joy that keeps.

The Lure of the Ocean's Heart

A whale in a tutu twirls with flair,
While clownfish jest without a care.
"Why so serious?" the eel would tease,
"Let's all swim by the dancing breeze!"

Anemones wiggle, put on a show,
While sea turtles race way too slow.
"Just keep it easy," the gulls would call,
As they dive down to catch the ball.

The pufferfish blows up for laughs,
"Oh look, I'm a balloon, no need for gaffs!"
The starfish giggles at every joke,
Swaying gently, as seaweed strokes.

So gather round, let joy be found,
In this deep blue world so laughter-bound.
With every splash, let humor chart,
The vibrant joy of the ocean's heart.

Lament of the Lost Currents

In waters deep, where fish do joke,
A current's lost, or just bespoke.
It swirled around, like lazy cats,
And left behind some funny hats.

The waves are wise, or so they say,
They giggle soft, then drift away.
With seaweed hair and barnacle shoes,
The tide's a prankster, spreading blues.

The starfish danced a wobbly jig,
While crabs all sang with voices big.
They played a tune on coral flutes,
And tapped their claws in playful suits.

Under the sea, where tall tales soar,
The fish will laugh forevermore.
So here we sit, on sandy floors,
With chuckles deep, and ocean roars.

Shadows in the Coral Garden

In coral caves, where shadows play,
The fish all laugh at the light of day.
A clownfish slips, a coral grin,
And giggles hide where laughs begin.

A seaweed wig, a playful sight,
Swirls by a jelly's silly flight.
The seahorses spin in a dizzy race,
While octopuses paint with a funny face.

They tickle the turtles, a slippery prank,
With bubbles bursting, the sea's a tank.
The sea cucumbers laugh with glee,
With wriggly bodies below the sea.

Here in the garden, bright and fleet,
The shadows dance on ticklish feet.
With laughter floating like sea foam,
In this ocean abode, they find their home.

Tides of Forgotten Memories

A clam once told a fishy tale,
Of waves that wear a funny veil.
The tide comes in with silly tricks,
And leaves us laughing by the bricks.

The sandcastles shaped like goofy hats,
Turn into homes for friendly rats.
As tides bring forth the lossy past,
They twirl and spin, they go so fast!

With shells that hum a tune so bright,
They party hard into the night.
Old barnacles join in the cheer,
And sing of stories we hold dear.

The moonlight casts a playful glow,
On waves that dance, and laughter flows.
In this ballet of tides we bask,
Forget the worries—no need to ask!

Beneath the Surface

Beneath the waves, the fun takes flight,
With critters having quite a night.
A shrimp held court, a tiny king,
While all his pals did laugh and sing.

The rocks would chuckle, the crabs would cheer,
With little fish swimming near.
They played hopscotch on the sand,
A wiggly game, all unplanned.

With sea cucumbers in a line,
They danced like hippos on some wine.
And every splash was met with joy,
A grand parade, not just a ploy!

So here we dwell in depths so deep,
Where laughter grows, and secrets heap.
In this ocean world, so bright and clear,
The fun spins round, come take a cheer!

Echoes Linger

In deep blue realms where gags abound,
The fish exchange jokes, all around.
They snicker loud, as currents swirl,
A comedy show, what a pearl!

With seahorses playing hide and seek,
In funny hats that make them peak.
Crabs scuttle off with quirky tunes,
Beneath the gaze of lazy moons.

With starfish holding star-studded fairs,
And jellyfish gliding in balloon pairs.
The ocean chuckles, a great big roar,
Reflections lost, yet fun galore!

So join the splash where laughter rings,
In watery halls where joy now clings.
For in these depths, the humor swims,
A playful jest that never dims.

Murmurs from the Abyss

A crab once tried to play a song,
But his pinch was way too strong.
He danced around with a silly cheer,
While fish all laughed, 'You're not so clear!'

A whale made bubbles, quite the sight,
Hiccuping tunes both day and night.
The dolphins gathered, all in a line,
Said, 'Dude, those bubbles are seriously fine!'

An octopus painted a mural bright,
But tripped on his own brush mid-flight.
The vibrant colors flew about,
While fish just laughed, 'Hey, what's that about?'

A clam played poker, with pearls to bet,
But he folded early, was that regret?
His friends just giggled, said, 'What a bore,
Next time, bring snacks, we want some more!'

Shadows Beneath the Waves

A starfish thought it could throw shade,
But it had no moves, just stuck and stayed.
It waved its arms with flair and grace,
While sea cucumbers laughed in place.

The jellyfish wiggled, a funky jam,
While squids joined in, shouting, 'Ma'am!'
But one got tangled in a wild dance,
And the other laughed, 'You lost your chance!'

A pufferfish tried to tell a joke,
But all he did was puff and choke.
The shrimp just cheered, 'You can't be serious!'
A fine fish tale, oh so mysterious!

A grouper wore shades, looking so cool,
Said, 'Check me out, I'm nobody's fool!'
But a lobster snickered, clapped with glee,
'Sorry dude, but you're still a sea!'

Songs of the Silent Depths

A clam sang softly, not quite a star,
Next to a seaweed playing guitar.
They broke into melodies, quite absurd,
While seahorses laughed, 'Have you heard?'

A fish in a tux tried to impress,
With a tap dance that was quite a mess.
He slipped and slid like a slippery bar,
And all the other fish said, 'How bizarre!'

A lonely conch, with a vintage tune,
Claimed it could serenade the moon.
But when it tried, it blew a rasp,
Leaving all sea critters gasping to gasp!

Anemones clapped with delight and cheer,
'Why don't we take our show up near?'
So they swam up and had a blast,
While waves of laughter echoed vast.

Currents of Forgotten Dreams

An old turtle dreamed of being fast,
While all the fish whizzed on past.
'Technique,' he said, 'is meant to be slow,'
And at that moment, he caught a glow.

A crab wore sneakers, feeling so spry,
But tripped on a rock, oh my, oh my!
His friends just chuckled, 'Stay in your shell,
Running is not what you do so well!'

A shrimp crafted wishes, made them fly,
With bubbles and sparkles that soared high.
But all they did was float and fizzle,
Leaving behind just a small drizzle.

A whale in a party hat took the floor,
With a wiggle and giggle, oh what a score!
A fish shouted, 'This is a sight to see!'
While others looked on, laughing with glee!

Reflections on a Sandy Canvas

Seagulls squawk in fancy hats,
Crabs dance around like silly diplomats.
A starfish plays the ukulele tune,
While jellyfish juggle under the moon.

Sandcastles topple with a swoosh,
As waves shout, 'Come join the push!'
A clam holds court, a noble stare,
While seashells gossip without a care.

Turtles race, but so slow and steady,
Each fin waving, are we ready?
Octopus chefs flipping seaweed fries,
As fish swim by with sparkly eyes.

In this quirky underwater fest,
Where laughter bubbles, we feel so blessed.
With every splash, our spirits soar,
In this realm where we laugh galore.

Depths of Forgotten Lore

Whales tell tales in whale-ish tones,
While sea cucumbers lie on their thrones.
Coral reefs wear their best disguise,
With mermaid gigs that mesmerize.

Pirates whisper, lost treasure near,
But it's just a shoe, dreadfully clear.
Pufferfish chuckle, all puffed and round,
As the ocean giggles without a sound.

Anemones flap like wild balloons,
Fishes parade to silly tunes.
With sand dollars laughing at the joke,
And krakens who only want to poke.

In this great blue, hilarity reigns,
From bubble-blowing to seaweed chains.
Under the waves, life's a comedy show,
Where legends dance, and laughter flows.

Tidal Whispers of Yesterday

A clam tells secrets with a wink,
As dolphins gather, they cheer and blink.
Tides giggle softly, rolling like glee,
While mermaids splash in a blue jubilee.

Seashells swap stories of days gone by,
Clownfish wear masks, giving laughs a try.
The ocean floor holds an annual fair,
With krill and plankton showing flair.

Sand dollars dream of flying high,
As bubbles pop with a sparkling sigh.
Lobsters dance in peculiar pairs,
A sight that leaves everyone in flares.

Through the waves, joy dances free,
In fluid laughter, we find our spree.
Under the sun, let hilarity fly,
In this world where the giggles never die.

Sailing Through Soundwaves

Bubbles burst with a silly sound,
As fishy musicians gather 'round.
A ship made of seaweed drifts along,
Swaying back to the ocean song.

Cranky crabs play shuffleboard,
With sea stars cheering every score.
Seahorses twist in a waltzing spree,
While sea urchins party wildly with glee.

Walruses wear their best tuxedo,
Sipping kelp smoothies at the casino.
Starfish do magic, flipping around,
While sea anemones groove to the sound.

In this bizarre maritime parade,
Where laughter and bubbles are carefully made.
Sailing through the splashes of joy,
In a currents' sway, we all employ.

Reflections in the Deep Blue

Fish in tuxedos dance with glee,
Bubble parties near a sea tree.
Octopus plays the drums all night,
With jellyfish softly glowing bright.

Seahorses giggle, wearing crowns,
As they parade through undersea towns.
Crabs in slippers shuffle by,
While snails are zooming, oh my, oh my!

Starfish tell jokes, they're quite the hit,
While gorging on snacks—a splendid fit.
Turtles laugh, say, "take it slow,"
As waves sing tunes, a vibrant show.

Down below, the whirligigs spin,
In this ocean, let's all dive in.
Mermaids chuckle, what a delight,
As fish turn cartwheels in sheer delight!

Windows into the Subaqueous

Through glassy panes, beneath the waves,
Sardines wiggle, oh how it braves!
Clownfish wear their colorful hats,
While whales call out for their lost mats.

Grouper's grinning, what a sight,
He cracks a joke, and it feels so right.
A sea cucumber starts to dance,
While nudibranchs take a flying chance!

Lobsters sport sunglasses, looking fine,
As they sip on algae-infused wine.
Coral reefs gossip, tales galore,
About the turtle who scooped the floor.

In this realm, laughter never ends,
Fishy friends break all the trends.
Dive on in, join the fun,
Where silliness reaps, and joy's never done!

Hushed Hymns of the Deep

In quiet tones, the sea life hums,
Whale choirs sing as a starfish drums.
Snakes of eels do a wiggly twist,
Witty remarks you won't want to miss.

Squids wearing shades wrap up the show,
While plankton giggle, putting on a glow.
A turtle winks, "Hey, I'm still cool!"
At the jellies swirling, it's quite the pool!

Rays of sunlight filter like confetti,
As bottom feeders bring their own spaghetti.
Lobsters boast of pearls they've found,
While sea urchins roll and spin around.

Deep down where the giggles swirl,
Life's a party, give it a twirl.
In this underwater world we adore,
Even the crabs can't help but roar!

Aquarius' Silent Lullaby

Beneath the surface, dreams take flight,
A dolphin's chuckle, a pure delight.
Starfish yawn, the day is done,
Ordering pizza from the deep, oh fun!

Pufferfish show off with a puff and a swell,
And sea otters giggle, can you tell?
With seaweed snacks, they munch and munch,
In this dreamy place, they love to bunch!

As bubbles rise, it's a light-hearted tale,
Of mermaids dancing, swishing their tail.
A crab complains of sand in his shoes,
On a journey to find the best ocean views.

So drift below, let laughter reign,
In the currents of joy, there's nothing mundane.
With stars above and waves so spry,
Join the merriment, oh my, oh my!

Beneath the Waves' Cloak

Bubbles rise with such grace,
Fish do a funny little race.
Mermaids giggle, a playful tease,
As crabs dance by with comical ease.

Seashells gossip in a shell-like tone,
Starfish lounge, they're never alone.
A whale sneezes, what a sight!
Octopus wears a hat, oh what a fright!

The seahorses play leapfrog around,
While jellyfish float without making a sound.
Dolphins squeak in a charming jest,
Making waves, they never rest.

In this realm where laughter lives,
Anemones tickle, oh how it gives!
Underneath this watery dome,
Life's a party in their vibrant home.

The Calm Before the Storm

Fish are yawning, oh what a sight,
As crabs dare each other to start a fight.
The sea is still, with a wink and a grin,
While barnacles huddle, pondering sin.

Seagulls are plotting a dive from above,
And lobsters are busy with veggies they love.
All creatures await the wild, wild ride,
With a splash of humor, they gather outside.

The breeze whispers jokes to everyone near,
While squids are cracking jokes, oh dear!
The tide's about to throw a wild bash,
And sea cucumbers are ready to splash!

Who knew that under the waves so wide,
Laughter and mischief are set to collide?
When the clouds gather, don't run for the shore,
Cause the wave before laughter opens the door!

Depths of Memory

Old sunken ships tell tales of the past,
While fish swim by, having a blast.
Ghostly pirates do a silly jig,
With a parrot that dances a tiny gig.

The corals play hide and seek with the tide,
As shells laugh quietly, full of pride.
An octopus swirls, with colors that beam,
In the currents, they float like a whimsical dream.

Starfish share secrets, in a splash of salt,
While turtles turn slow, never at fault.
Anemones chuckle, their arms flailing wide,
In the depths of the sea, there's joy inside.

So when memories bubble from distant shores,
Know that laughter resides in the undulating roars.
Among the treasures where sunlight can't reach,
Is a carnival of giggles that hope to teach.

Requiem for the Undercurrents

In swirling depths where shadows play,
A fish philosopher has something to say.
He muses on bubbles that never come clear,
While remoras giggle, they have no fear.

Sardines are practicing synchronized dances,
While lobsters plot terrible prances.
The undercurrents hum a silly tune,
As clams share stories beneath the moon.

Eels slither by, in sequins so bright,
Swaying to rhythms that feel just right.
Crabs make wisecracks, their shells clapping loud,
While everything laughs, like it's under a shroud.

In the whirl of waters, a tale's spun anew,
Where antics abound, and laughter breaks through.
So let's raise a glass to the sea's quirky mates,
For under the surface, life's full of jests and fates.

www.ingramcontent.com/pod-product-compliance
Lightning Source LLC
Chambersburg PA
CBHW062108280426
43661CB00086B/335